LIFE'S LITTLE
INSTRUCTION
BOOK

summersdale

LIFE'S LITTLE INSTRUCTION BOOK

Summersdale Publishers Ltd
46 West Street
Chichester
West Sussex
PO19 1RP
UK

www.summersdale.com

Printed and bound in Croatia

ISBN: 978-1-78685-036-2

Substantial discounts on bulk quantities of Summersdale books are available to corporations, professional associations and other organisations. For details contact general enquiries: telephone: +44 (0) 1243 771107 or email: enquiries@summersdale.com.

INSTRUCTIONS FOR LIVING A LIFE. PAY ATTENTION. BE ASTONISHED. TELL ABOUT IT.

MARY OLIVER

WAKE UP WITH THE SUNRISE...

◆

... and if you can't, use a 'wake up light'! This nifty device simulates the dawn, gently rousing you from sleep before your alarm can shock you awake.

GET UP AND GO

◆

Hitting the snooze button feels good but can confuse your brain into not sending its 'wake up' signals, such as raising your core temperature. Instead, embrace the short-term pain for the sake of long-term gain – get out of that bed!

MAKE YOUR BED

◆

Do Future You a favour and
turn the covers back for fifteen
minutes to air out your sheets,
then make your bed so it's all neat
and tidy. Those smooth sheets
are going to feel so good when
you climb in between them.

LIFE IS TEN PER CENT
WHAT HAPPENS TO YOU
AND NINETY PER CENT
HOW YOU RESPOND TO IT.

LOU HOLTZ

BREAKFAST LIKE ROYALTY

◆

This isn't a myth made up by your mum; having a big breakfast really gets you off to a good start. It can boost your mood, boost your concentration and it's healthier than skipping it altogether.

BRUSH YOUR TONGUE WITH A TOOTHBRUSH

◆

Two words for you: tongue bacteria.
Another two words for you:
bad breath. A final three words
for you: brush your tongue.

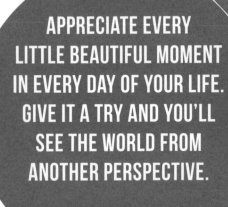

**APPRECIATE EVERY
LITTLE BEAUTIFUL MOMENT
IN EVERY DAY OF YOUR LIFE.
GIVE IT A TRY AND YOU'LL
SEE THE WORLD FROM
ANOTHER PERSPECTIVE.**

THEA KRISTINE MAY

INSTIGATE A 'FIVE-MINUTE FLAP' RULE

◆

Aim to be ready five minutes before you need to leave. You won't need it most days, but when you lose your keys, forget your lunch or spill tea on your clean shirt, those spare five minutes will be invaluable.

HEART YOUR HEART!

◆

When you insert a little exercise into
your morning routine you give a
little love to your heart and lungs.
Can you cycle to the station? Walk
to get a morning paper? Take the
stairs instead of the lift?
Do it.

LOVE YOUR FELLOW COMMUTERS, EVEN IF YOU HATE THEM

◆

We tend to judge ourselves by our intentions and others by their actions. Try to ascribe the best possible intentions to strangers. The person who cut you up at the junction might have an emergency. Or they might not, but getting angry only spoils your own morning.

LISTEN TO
YOUR STOMACH

◆

No, not about having a snack. You've
just had breakfast. But as you
start your morning's endeavours,
check in with your body. An ache
in your stomach or tension in
your neck may mean that you're
not happy with what you're doing
and need to consider a change.

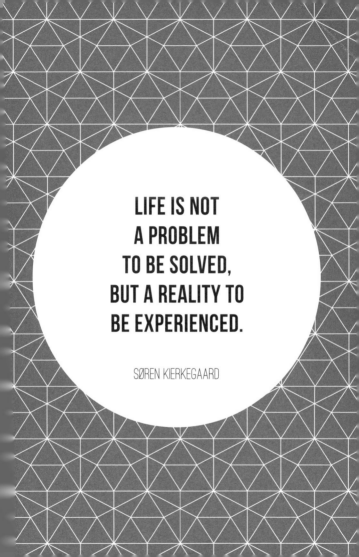

LIFE IS NOT
A PROBLEM
TO BE SOLVED,
BUT A REALITY TO
BE EXPERIENCED.

SØREN KIERKEGAARD

CHANT-RA
YOUR MANTRA

◆

Every day contains its little
challenges. A mantra that affirms
your core beliefs or responses can
really help you fortify yourself. Even
a childish 'I am rubber, you are
glue' can lend you some strength
in tricky situations – just remember
to say it under your breath.

LOVE YOUR LITTLE TOE

◆

If you're struggling with self-esteem, start small and work your way up. Find something you like about yourself, even if it's only a tiny part of you, and note it daily. Mindfully noting your positive attributes can open your heart to other parts of yourself.

DO NOT GO WHERE
THE PATH MAY LEAD;
GO INSTEAD WHERE
THERE IS NO PATH
AND LEAVE A TRAIL.

RALPH WALDO EMERSON

EAT A RAINBOW
(OF FRUIT AND VEG)

◆

Look, only Perfect Humans find it easy to eat a healthy amount of fruit and veg. Beat the pain of getting your seven-a-day (that's right, it's seven now) and try to eat something in every colour of the rainbow.

BEND BEFORE
YOU BREAK

◆

Unless you are James Bond defusing
a bomb on a rapid countdown,
it is A-OK to take a break from a
tricky and important problem.
Walk away. Have a cup of tea.
Complete a simple task to regain
your confidence. Now you can
return to your task refreshed.

NO IS A COMPLETE SENTENCE, SO SAY IT

◆

Not only is it acceptable to say you can't take on a task or attend an event, you can say it without providing a dissertation on why. Simply say 'I'm afraid I can't attend/ take that on' and then apologise or offer a different schedule.

WHOLE-ASS IT, DON'T HALF-ASS IT

◆

If you don't have the time to do something right the first time, you won't have the time to bring it up to scratch later. Do it with all your energy and focus and do it now.

TAKE CHANCES, MAKE MISTAKES. THAT'S HOW YOU GROW. PAIN NOURISHES YOUR COURAGE. YOU HAVE TO FAIL IN ORDER TO PRACTISE BEING BRAVE.

MARY TYLER MOORE

NOTHING LOOKS AS GOOD AS COMFORTABLE FEELS

◆

Society demands that you wear clothes at all times while in public. That's too much time to be wearing uncomfortable clothes, even if they are the most beautiful trousers in the world. Beautiful things don't pinch you in the thigh, and that's a fact.

ALWAYS HAVE
THE FACTS

◆

It's good to believe what you
are saying, but it's better to
know what you are saying.
Look into the facts you hear,
investigate the assumptions you
are making and be clear when
you're not sure on something.

LOVE ALL,
TRUST A FEW,
DO WRONG TO NONE.

WILLIAM SHAKESPEARE

USE YOUR BUDGET – IT'S A SATNAV FOR YOUR MONEY

◆

What's your destination? Savings? A holiday? Being debt-free? Having a budget directs your money towards that and stops it veering off into fields full of expensive sandwiches or unworn shoes.

ASSUME YOU'RE WEARING AN INVISIBILITY CLOAK

◆

Quick challenge: describe all the strangers you've seen today. I bet you can't come up with more than one or two. Don't be self-conscious when out in public because it's likely that everyone that you think is judging you hasn't even noticed you.

COMPETE WITH YOURSELF, NOT OTHERS

◆

It's good to recognise the positive traits in others, and to aspire to better yourself, but don't get the two mixed up. You should only aspire to be a better version of you.

WORK, PLAY AND SLEEP IN EQUAL MEASURE

◆

There are 24 hours in a day –
that's eight hours for working,
eight hours to laugh, sing, read,
run, learn, talk, breathe... and eight
hours for a luxurious night's sleep
to process the goodness of the day.

WHEN YOU ARE
CONTENT TO BE SIMPLY
YOURSELF AND DON'T
COMPARE OR COMPETE,
EVERYBODY WILL
RESPECT YOU.

LAO TZU

NATURE IS MEDICINE FOR YOUR SOUL...

◆

... and for your body. Spending time in nature can combat stress, fatigue, improve short-term memory and combat inflammation. Besides, isn't it wonderful to remember we live in such a beautiful world?

TAKE IT OFF TO
SHAKE IT OFF

◆

The first step of your daytime to
evening transformation should be
to change from your uniform or
'getting things done' clothes and into
relaxing, comfortable leisure wear. It
will refresh you and give you a sense
of transitioning from 'on' to 'relaxed'.

ADD A SPOONFUL OF SUGAR TO YOUR COOKING

◆

Cooking isn't fun for everyone, but it is necessary – you can't live on takeaways forever. Introduce a podcast, audiobook or even an app like language learning to your cooking time to make it something to look forward to.

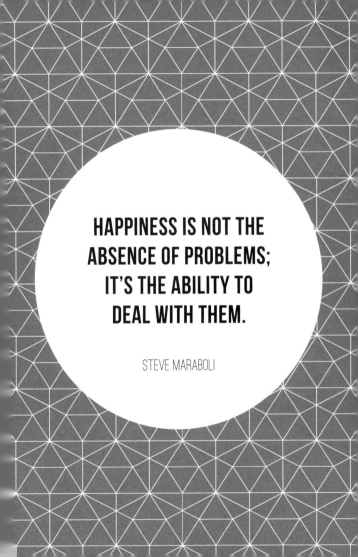

HAPPINESS IS NOT THE
ABSENCE OF PROBLEMS;
IT'S THE ABILITY TO
DEAL WITH THEM.

STEVE MARABOLI

ADD A SPRINKLE OF SALT TO YOUR COOKING TOO

◆

Seasoning your dish is one of
the best things you can do for
your flavourings. When you cook,
have some sea salt and a pepper
grinder on hand at all times,
so you can season to taste.

NEVER WEAR WHITE WHILE COOKING

◆

It doesn't matter how careful you are, food will find its way onto your clothing and it will stain.

THERE ARE TWO WAYS OF SPREADING LIGHT: TO BE THE CANDLE, OR THE MIRROR THAT REFLECTS IT.

EDITH WHARTON

UNWIND AND UNPLUG BEFORE BED

◆

Before you go to bed, give yourself 30 minutes of relaxation. No screens, no stimuli, just gently going about your evening tasks and winding down from the day. You will sleep better.

RESERVE YOUR BED FOR SLEEP AND SEX

◆

Getting into bed should fill you with delicious anticipation, although for what depends on your mood. It should be free of any feeling of chores or daily concerns and be a pure source of happiness. Plus, this keeps the pillow fresh on your cheek!

LEARN LIKE YOU WILL BE ALIVE FOREVER!

◆

There are so many fascinating things you could teach yourself about, and it's never been easier to learn a new skill or brush up on your knowledge. Absorbing new information stimulates our minds, too, so always have a challenge to work on.

LET THE LITTLE THINGS GO

◆

Will you look back years from now and still be upset about that time your friend cancelled your plans, or that time you couldn't find a parking spot? Didn't think so. It is useful to learn to let smaller burdens disappear.

WORRY PRETENDS
TO BE NECESSARY
BUT SERVES NO
USEFUL PURPOSE.

ECKHART TOLLE

THE SKY'S THE LIMIT... BUT YOU HAVE TO STRETCH UP TO REACH IT

◆

Nothing is given to you on a plate. Yes, you can do wonderful things, but you'll only get there through hard work.

BE A SPONGE!

◆

Explore your world and stay
curious. Embrace the natural
human instinct to be intrigued
by everything you see.

KEEP MAKING
REALISTIC GOALS

◆

Set yourself new, attainable goals often, and reward yourself for the ones that you accomplish along the way. Each practical goal will give you a boost of accomplishment and bring you one step closer to fulfilling your wildest dreams.

WHEN YOU STOP
EXPECTING PEOPLE
TO BE PERFECT, YOU
CAN LIKE THEM FOR
WHO THEY ARE.

DONALD MILLER

LIVE LIFE IN THE SLOW LANE

◆

Pay attention to your mind and
body: they know when you
need to be active, and when
you need to stop and chill out
and have some down time.

CHOOSE YOUR WORDS CAREFULLY

◆

A hasty response can sometimes come off badly to your recipients. Check over what you have written to see how you have expressed yourself. Take your time to think about your word choice and even the way you've punctuated a sentence to make sure your point can't be misconstrued.

WE UNDERESTIMATE
THE POWER OF A SMILE,
A KIND WORD, A LISTENING
EAR, AN HONEST
COMPLIMENT, OR THE
SMALLEST ACT OF CARING.

LEO BUSCAGLIA

MAKE YOUR FRIENDS THE FAMILY YOU CHOOSE

◆

In the age of social media and
hundreds of online friends
and 'followers', make the
effort to cultivate deep and
supportive friendships.

SPEND TIME FIRST
AND MONEY SECOND

Time is the most precious
currency there is. Spend it on
your most precious people, in
person and without distractions.

BE AN ACTIVE LISTENER

◆

This one is easy and very effective.
Listen closely to what your friend
or loved one is saying. When
responding, avoid shifting the focus
back to your opinion or position
and continue to engage with their
point of view. It makes people
feel good to be truly heard.

IF YOU GET TO CUT THE CAKE, THE OTHER PERSON GETS TO CHOOSE THEIR SLICE

◆

Make arrangements that give people the power to choose – playing fair isn't just for children!

WE MAKE A LIVING BY
WHAT WE GET,
BUT WE MAKE A LIFE
BY WHAT WE GIVE.

WINSTON CHURCHILL

NEVER LEND
SOMETHING YOU
NEED BACK

◆

If you don't want to lose a friend
over a misplaced item of sentimental
value, or tricky money issues,
never lend anything that you can't
afford to see gone forever.

ASK YOURSELF, 'IS THIS THE HILL I WANT TO DIE ON?'

◆

This sounds pretty harsh, but really, is this one particular issue the one that's worth ending your friendship over? Even if the apology wasn't quite the wording you'd like or you still don't agree who started it, isn't it worth letting it go?

**POSITIVE ENERGY
IS ATTRACTED TO
POSITIVE ENERGY.**

DEBORAH DAY

IF SOMEONE TELLS YOU WHO THEY ARE, BELIEVE THEM

◆

For example, if a friend is always chronically late, then accept that as a personality trait. You can create strategies to help manage your interactions with them, or else consider if it's something you can't bear and act upon that, but don't try to change them.

DON'T SET YOURSELF ON FIRE TO KEEP SOMEONE ELSE WARM

◆

It's good to help friends and family, but it's also good to make sure you are OK too. If a friend asks for help and you think it will be too much to lend a hand, it's fine to say 'not at the moment'.

YOUR FEELINGS SHOULD BE A STREAM, NOT A DAM

◆

If someone has hurt you, go ahead and tell them how you feel. Communication is half the battle. But be prepared for your feelings to change – you may not feel the same way after a few days, and that's OK.

GIVE AWAY A GOOD THOUGHT A DAY

◆

Do you like someone's shoes?
Tell them. Did you see something
funny and think of someone? Pass it
on! It feels so good to know we are
in someone else's heart and mind.

MY MISSION IN LIFE
IS NOT MERELY TO SURVIVE,
BUT TO THRIVE; AND TO DO
SO WITH SOME PASSION,
SOME COMPASSION, SOME
HUMOUR AND SOME STYLE.

MAYA ANGELOU

MAKE YOUR PASSION
YOUR CAREER

Find out what you love,
and then find a way to make
your passion your job.

YOU DON'T HAVE TO AGREE WITH SOMEONE TO LOVE THEM

◆

Don't make your friendship conditional on agreeing on every single topic. It can be fun to have calm debates on certain subjects. It's also absolutely fine to have subjects that you don't discuss.

ALWAYS BE A LITTLE KINDER THAN IS NECESSARY

◆

Every journey through life is different; each has its own delays, bridges and obstacles – you never know what someone else is going through, or what effect your words or actions can have on others. Kindness costs nothing, and everyone is deserving of it.

VERY LITTLE IS NEEDED
TO MAKE A HAPPY LIFE;
IT IS ALL WITHIN YOURSELF,
IN YOUR WAY OF THINKING.

MARCUS AURELIUS

IF YOU WANT TO BE HAPPY, SPEND YOUR TIME WITH HAPPY PEOPLE

◆

Happy energy is infectious. To gain a positive attitude, surround yourself with people that are full of light and laughter. There is nothing more powerful than joy.

LISTEN MORE THAN YOU TALK

◆

Listening to other people can teach us more than we'll ever know from speaking. Everyone has a story to tell; every life has something that you can learn from. Be quiet every once in a while and let others speak.

FRIENDSHIPS NEED TO BE NURTURED

◆

Friendships don't build themselves. Take some time out of your busy schedule and find a moment to have a cuppa or a phone call with an old friend, or be the one to suggest an activity with a new one – it will always be appreciated.

CREATE A TRIBE

◆

Introduce friends to each other.
With several companions in
common it makes it easier
to maintain and strengthen
friendships for all of you, and you'll
experience the joy of watching
people you love create bonds.

LOVE SOMEONE
THEIR WAY

◆

If you think the most romantic
thing in the world is to receive
flowers and your partner thinks
the most romantic thing in
the world is to receive regular
compliments, ask for the flowers
but always give the compliments.

I'VE LEARNED THAT BEING KIND IS MORE IMPORTANT THAN BEING RIGHT.

H. JACKSON BROWN JR

IF YOU FALL IN LOVE, CHOOSE TO STAY IN LOVE

◆

Always put time and effort into your relationship. Date each other, keep the compliments flowing and always be thinking of new ways to make your loved one happy.

A DATE A WEEK KEEPS THE RELATIONSHIP AT ITS PEAK

◆

Reserve one day a week to spend
quality time with each other, just
the two of you. Having a schedule
for romance might not seem
too dreamy, but it helps you
make your partner a priority.

SHARE THE GOOD;
SHARE THE BAD

◆

If one person in a relationship has
an issue, both people should be
working together to solve it.
It can be anything from someone
taking a little more housework
when their partner is struggling at
work, to both of you sitting down
and working out a plan to help
each other achieve your dreams.

NEVER SPEAK IN ANGER

◆

You can't undo cruel words,
even if you're very sorry about
them. A calm, considered
disagreement should always be
your top argument priority.

ANYONE WHO KEEPS
LEARNING STAYS YOUNG.
THE GREATEST THING
IN LIFE IS TO KEEP
YOUR MIND YOUNG.

HENRY FORD

IT SHOULD ALWAYS BE YOU VS THE PROBLEM, NOT YOU VS YOUR LOVED ONE

◆

Can't agree on budgeting or mealtime etiquette? Sit down with your loved one and ask them, 'what can I do to help resolve this?'

YOU MIGHT FORGIVE AND FORGET, BUT YOUR BEST FRIEND WON'T

◆

Be careful when venting about
your lover to friends. It feels good
and helps you to forgive and
forget, but if you only ever say
bad things, your friends will find it
hard to shake a bad impression.

LEARN SOMETHING NEW EVERY DAY

◆

Take on projects and go to classes
with a friend or partner. Not only
will learning something new keep
the relationship fresh, but you
have the pleasure of working
together as a team and sharing
experiences with each other.

**MANY OF LIFE'S
FAILURES ARE PEOPLE
WHO DID NOT REALISE
HOW CLOSE THEY WERE
TO SUCCESS WHEN
THEY GAVE UP.**

THOMAS EDISON

DON'T JUST KNOW YOUR LOVER, LEARN YOUR LOVER

◆

Everyone changes, even those we've known for years. Keep in touch with your partner's likes and dislikes and ask their opinion even if you think you know it.

NEVER GO TO BED ON AN ARGUMENT

◆

Leaving hot feelings to fester
overnight only prolongs a
negativity that could otherwise
have been solved sooner.

YOU CAN, YOU SHOULD,
AND IF YOU'RE BRAVE
ENOUGH TO START,
YOU WILL.

STEPHEN KING

LOVE IS NOT ALWAYS EASY; SOMETIMES YOU HAVE TO WORK AT IT

◆

Relationships aren't nearly as cheesy or plain sailing as they seem to be in the films. It takes compromise, consideration, communication, respect, honesty and actual effort – it's not going to be wonderful all by itself.

BE WITH SOMEONE WHO MAKES YOU LAUGH

◆

Laughing together releases
endorphins, which not only
make you feel good but will also
strengthen your attraction to your
partner. If it's your significant
other who is the one to make
you laugh, even better – you
have something truly special.

FIND SOMEONE WHO MAKES YOU FEEL EASY TO LOVE

◆

Anyone that makes you feel like you are hard to love is not right for you. The right person will embrace you for everything you are – flaws included.

NO RELATIONSHIP
IS PERFECT

◆

Never compare your relationship
to someone else's. Even if someone
you know seems to have the perfect
romance, you don't know what goes
on behind closed doors; everyone
has ups and downs just like you.

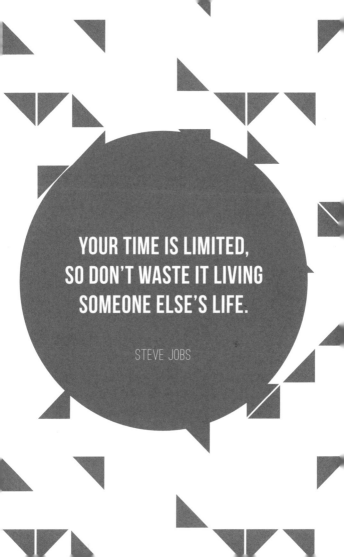

YOUR TIME IS LIMITED,
SO DON'T WASTE IT LIVING
SOMEONE ELSE'S LIFE.

STEVE JOBS

YOU DON'T HAVE TO LOVE YOUR PARTNER'S LOVES

◆

It's OK if your partner likes golf on Sundays and you like tennis, and you shouldn't worry if you find what they love most just plain boring; difference is often a healthy thing. Develop a balance of interests; some to share and some that are separate.

VENT TO YOUR DRAFTS BOX

◆

In times of conflict write an email
to the person involved expressing
all of your thoughts and feelings;
save it (don't press send!) and give
it some time. If you still want to
send it after that, go ahead: time
is powerful and can give some
much-needed perspective.
You might not feel the same
about things once you have
let the air cool down.

NEVER BE TOO GOOD TO START AT THE BOTTOM

◆

All jobs include some less-fun tasks, and starting positions seem to include more than most. Knowing everything there is about your job and your company is just a tactical advantage, so view it as a challenge, and don't turn your nose up at any opportunity.

HAVE ONE DAY
OF PAIN FOR A
YEAR OF GAINS

◆

Set aside one day to automate all your financial dealings, including setting a budgeted amount that goes straight into your savings account on pay day. That way, you've saved the money before you've had a chance to spend it.

THERE IS ONLY ONE THING
THAT MAKES A DREAM
IMPOSSIBLE TO ACHIEVE:
THE FEAR OF FAILURE.

PAULO COELHO

PUT YOUR HAND UP, YOU NEVER KNOW WHO WILL TAKE IT

◆

Volunteer for jobs where you
can. Say yes if someone asks for
help. You'll be seen as keen, it will
add variety to your day and you
never know where it will lead.

IF YOU CAN LAUGH TOGETHER, YOU CAN WORK TOGETHER

◆

The best teams really start coming
together when you can feel at
ease in each other's company.
After all, these are the people you
spend most of your day with!

IF YOU'RE WILLING TO WORK AT IT, YOU CAN RAPIDLY IMPROVE THE QUALITY OF EVERY PART OF YOUR LIFE.

BRIAN TRACY

BECOME A
BUSINESS PICASSO

◆

Once you know your job,
it's time to think about
how you can improve it.
Everyone has times when
they've thought, 'this would
be much smoother if...'
Would it save the company time
or money? Then write to your
boss and suggest your idea.

THERE'S NO SUCH THING AS 'OVER-PREPARED'

◆

Whether you're working on a project or about to have an important meeting, memorise the essential information and have a folder of extra research on hand. That way you expect the unexpected.

HAVE A TO-DO LIST

◆

Simple as it may sound, writing
a to-do list is a fool-proof way to
become more organised. Your
tasks for the day are visible and
encourage you to allocate time slots
and make priorities. Plus it feels
great when you tick items off!

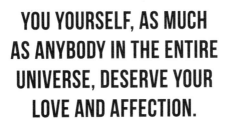

YOU YOURSELF, AS MUCH
AS ANYBODY IN THE ENTIRE
UNIVERSE, DESERVE YOUR
LOVE AND AFFECTION.

BUDDHA

FENG-SHUI YOUR OFFICE SPACE

◆

Desk space is important for your working life: the stuff on your desk could be cluttering your mind, so clear it. Make your office somewhere you want to be and introduce some greenery, have relevant books by your computer, keep it tidy and you'll feel more at peace with being at work.

MAKE YESTERDAY'S WEAKNESS TODAY'S STRENGTH

◆

Maybe presenting to large groups or organisation isn't your forte. Make it your challenge for the year; research ways to improve, practice and ask your place of work to train you in that area.

THE PAST IS A FOREIGN COUNTRY; THEY DO THINGS DIFFERENTLY THERE.

J. P. HARTLEY

BE THE TYPE OF PERSON YOU'D WANT YOUR CHILD TO MARRY

◆

Everyone is someone's son or daughter, and their parents want the best for them. Treat everyone with the respect they deserve.

NEVER LEAVE SCHOOL

◆

Learning your job is as important as performing it. Schedule time every week to read up on the industry, look into training opportunities or read research in your area.
This way you'll be able to keep an eye on what your competitors are doing and you'll be spotting the most up to date trends that will give you plenty of new ideas.

ASSERT YOURSELF

◆

In the workplace it is important
to make yourself heard. Let your
thoughts and ideas be known, and
communicate your limits and needs.

FLIP YOUR ROUTINE

◆

General admin and email responses
might be how we generally start
our days, but in fact it is better to
begin with a creative task when
our minds are fresh. Try shaking
up your daily work routine and
see if you find it rewarding.

WHATEVER YOU WANT TO
DO, DO IT NOW; THERE ARE
ONLY SO MANY TOMORROWS.

MICHAEL LANDON

STRETCH

◆

At least once every hour you spend sitting at a desk, turn your screen off and perform small stretches for a few minutes. You'll feel rejuvenated and help to alleviate any back and neck problems further down the line.

PUT THE FUN BACK IN 'EXERCISE IS FUNDAMENTAL AND THERE'S NO WAY TO GET OUT OF IT, SORRY'

◆

You'd better find something you enjoy because there's really no other option than to exercise three times a week. Try a club or a class.

BALANCE YOUR PLATE

◆

Eating good, balanced food will keep you energised for longer. Fill half of your dish with leafy greens and vegetables; no more than one quarter should be grains or legumes: brown rice, lentils, black beans, etc. and the last quarter should be healthy protein: eggs, legumes, seeds or grilled meat or fish.

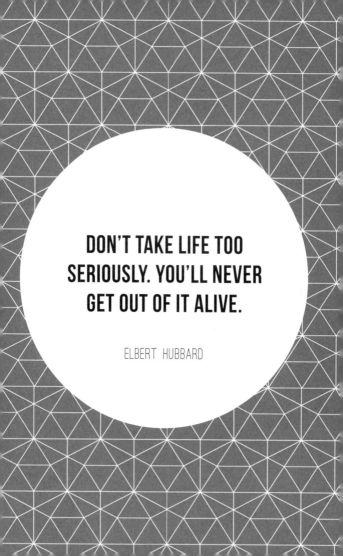

DON'T TAKE LIFE TOO SERIOUSLY. YOU'LL NEVER GET OUT OF IT ALIVE.

ELBERT HUBBARD

THERE ARE NO BADDIES IN FOOD, ONLY MORALLY COMPLEX CHARACTERS

◆

Fat is not the enemy: think avocados, almonds, seeds, olive oil for salads and coconut oil for cooking. Fats like these will give you glowing skin, great hair and a boosted immune system.

REHYDRATE, DON'T DEHYDRATE!

◆

Drinking more water can ease fatigue, even boost energy; it gets rid of headaches, flushes out toxins and reinforces your immune system. Halve your weight in pounds to get the amount of water you should be drinking per day in ounces.

YOU CAN BE THE RIPEST,
JUICIEST PEACH IN THE
WORLD, BUT THERE WILL
ALWAYS BE SOMEONE
WHO HATES PEACHES.

DITA VON TEESE

SLEEPING IS COOL AGAIN

◆

It's all about the late nights and the heavy mornings when you're young, but when you want to feel good, snoozing is where it's at! A healthy adult needs between seven and nine hours' sleep a day – listen to what your body is telling you and adjust accordingly.

THINK OUTSIDE
THE BOX

◆

TV isn't all bad, but becoming immersed in too much television can leave us feeling a little deflated. Whenever you reach for the remote, think again – craft, play a game, call a friend, cook or do something else you enjoy.

UP YOUR
SNACKING GAME

◆

Snacking is great, and healthy grazing can help stop hunger pangs (which in turn can lead to binge eating) so up your snacking game! Slice some of your favourite exotic fruit, fill up on a bag of mixed nuts and freeze some of your own low-fat yoghurt.

WHEREVER YOU GO,
NO MATTER WHAT THE
WEATHER, ALWAYS BRING
YOUR OWN SUNSHINE.

ANTHONY J. D'ANGELO

YOU'RE NOT A VAMPIRE (YET)

◆

We develop vitamin D when we spend time in the sun's light, so go outside and catch some rays. Spend at least ten minutes a day in the sunlight to improve your mood and strengthen your bones.

COOK FROM SCRATCH

Most of the time the 'jar'll do'
approach is quick, simple and easy;
however ready-made food comes
at a sugary price. Cooking from
scratch can be rewarding both
for your mind and your body.

KEEP A PERSONAL FOOD BANK

◆

Learn at least three quick and tasty meals you can make from scratch and always have the ingredients on hand. Try tomato pasta, vegetable stir fry and cheese omelette to start.

EDUCATED FOOD

◆

Read the small print on your food.
It might sound time consuming and
a bit fussy, but you'll be surprised
at what goes into some of what
you buy. It'll give you a better
idea of what you are putting into
your body and perhaps guide
you towards healthier choices.

IT IS THE WAY ONE TREATS
HIS INFERIORS MORE THAN
THE WAY HE TREATS HIS
EQUALS WHICH REVEALS
ONE'S REAL CHARACTER.

CHARLES BAYARD MILIKEN

GROW YOUR OWN

◆

It doesn't have to be a garden dedicated to growing veg; start off small and grow the herbs you like in your curry or the tomatoes in your salad. Not only is it better for the planet, but cultivating a living thing can boost your mood and self-esteem too!

EAT LESS MEAT

◆

Get creative with your meals and begin the week with healthy habits by not eating meat on a Monday. Meat production is one of the biggest problems facing the environment, and every opportunity we take to reduce our meat consumption helps the planet. Plus, eating more veg (and in more interesting ways) is always a good idea.

A SMART PERSON
KNOWS HOW TO TALK.
A WISE PERSON KNOWS
WHEN TO BE SILENT.

ROY T. BENNETT

CHANGE WHAT YOU CAN, WHEN YOU WANT TO

◆

Don't just sit there being annoyed
or frustrated – fix the buzzing light,
walk away from the noisy cougher
or even leave the bad film.

THERE ARE ALWAYS NEW PATHS TO BE FOUND, OR CREATED

◆

Picture life being like a forest: the paths we want to take can often seem unclear but when you're at a turning point, sometimes all it takes is to step back, look around you, and strike out a new pathway through the trees.

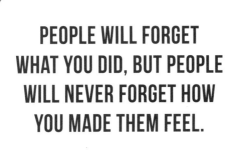

PEOPLE WILL FORGET
WHAT YOU DID, BUT PEOPLE
WILL NEVER FORGET HOW
YOU MADE THEM FEEL.

MAYA ANGELOU

SAVOUR THE
FOOD YOU EAT

◆

On the way to work we might
grab a coffee, or at lunch steal a
moment for a takeaway sandwich,
but eating food 'on the run' means
that we are not appreciating its
taste or goodness. Food and drink
are some of life's greatest pleasures
so make the time to enjoy them.

ALWAYS SLEEP ON AN IMPULSE DECISION

◆

If you want to buy something unusually expensive, walk away from the shop or save it in your basket, and sleep on it. If you still want it in a week, then you want it enough!

I ALWAYS PREFER TO BELIEVE THE BEST OF EVERYBODY; IT SAVES SO MUCH TROUBLE.

RUDYARD KIPLING

TURN STUMBLING BLOCKS INTO STEPPING STONES AND SKIP YOUR WAY TO THE OTHER SIDE

◆

Every problem you face is a stepping stone that leads to greater things – you learn so much from every difficulty in life, and never know where it might lead. So next time you approach an obstacle, see it as a challenge, that when tackled may lead to better things.

IF YOU DON'T HAVE TIME TO GET IT RIGHT NOW, YOU WON'T HAVE TIME TO FIX IT LATER

◆

This doesn't mean you have to be perfect all the time. It means you should perform a task as completely as possible and with all your ability.

DON'T BE IN
SUCH A HURRY

◆

Time is fast enough. Don't wish
it all away so quickly; life is best
experienced at a slower pace.

A BAD TIME IS A GOOD STORY WAITING TO HAPPEN

◆

When something is going particularly
awry and you just have to get
through it, start to think on how
you'll retell this in the future.
You'll stop focussing on the pain
and start thinking of things as
an opportunity for comedy.

THE WOMAN WHO WALKS
ALONE IS LIKELY TO FIND
HERSELF IN PLACES NO
ONE HAS BEEN BEFORE.

ALBERT EINSTEIN

WEAR WHAT YOU HAVE AND QUIT BUYING MORE

◆

Most people own more clothes than they will ever wear. If an item of clothing doesn't make you feel great, pass it on to a friend or charity shop. Remember why you loved old favourites in the first place and wear them with pride.

IT'S THE SIMPLE THINGS IN LIFE THAT ARE THE MOST EXTRAORDINARY

◆

Take pleasure in the simplicities of life; they are often the most beautiful. It's not always about the fireworks but more so the quiet walks in the park, or a good book.

MAY I NEVER BE COMPLETE.
MAY I NEVER BE CONTENT.
MAY I NEVER BE PERFECT.

CHUCK PALAHNIUK

APPRECIATE
YOUR SKILLS

◆

If you're worried your education
or job history isn't killing it on
your CV, sit down and write a
list of everything you're able
to do well. With a touch of
rewriting, you'll find many of
these can be put on your CV.

FORMAL EDUCATION IS IMPORTANT, BUT NOT NECESSARY

◆

Life can be an education in itself so live it exactly the way you want to and don't forget that in life there are many paths to the same successes.

LEFTOVERS ARE A MAN'S BEST FRIEND

◆

There are too many people out there who don't have the same luxuries as you. Freeze leftovers for another day rather than throw them out, and only buy what you know you will eat.

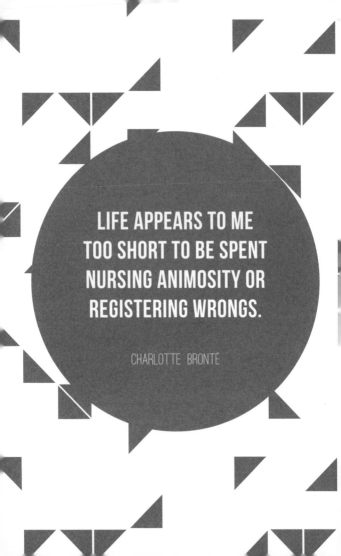

LIFE APPEARS TO ME
TOO SHORT TO BE SPENT
NURSING ANIMOSITY OR
REGISTERING WRONGS.

CHARLOTTE BRONTË

WHEN ONE DOOR CLOSES, ACCEPT THAT IT'S SHUT AND FIND ANOTHER

◆

Life is way too short to waste time knocking on a door that we know is locked; try another one!

MAKE A 'CHANGE THE WORLD' BUDGET

◆

Pick two causes you care
passionately about and arrange
a direct debit to transfer
£5 to them monthly.

A TEACHER IS A CLEVER STUDENT

◆

The more knowledge that you explore, the more you find to know. There are plenty of free or inexpensive lectures, workshops and community events where you can pick up skills and information.

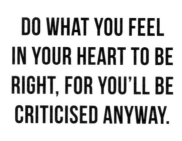

DO WHAT YOU FEEL
IN YOUR HEART TO BE
RIGHT, FOR YOU'LL BE
CRITICISED ANYWAY.

ELEANOR ROOSEVELT

LIFE IS NOT ALWAYS FAIR

◆

Sometimes things just aren't fair or even right. Circumstances can arise that may have no explanation for how or why they occur, but it is better for us to accept those things and move on than to waste time complaining.

MAKE YOUR DECISIONS WITH CERTAINTY

◆

Worrying about the infinite possibilities of what *could* go wrong can make a person never actually make a decision at all. Be confident in your decision – after all, if your plan doesn't work out, you can always try again.

IT IS ONLY WITH THE HEART
THAT ONE CAN SEE RIGHTLY;
WHAT IS ESSENTIAL IS
INVISIBLE TO THE EYE.

ANTOINE DE SAINT-EXUPÉRY

ASK YOURSELF, IS THIS KIND, IS THIS TRUE, IS THIS NECESSARY?

◆

Seriously, is what you're about to say going to make you and your listener feel good or bad? Hate only hurts the hater – holding on to resentment is like drinking poison and expecting the other person to die. Choose not to speak if the only outcome will be negativity.

DON'T BE AFRAID TO ASK

◆

You secretly want the last
piece of cake. Well, just ask!
Otherwise later you will be sitting
in bed wondering how the last
piece would have tasted.

LIFE IS
HAPPENING NOW

◆

Be completely present in a
moment to get the most out of it.
Give the present moment your
whole attention, whether you're
appreciating the warmth of a
shower, chatting to a loved one,
savouring a meal or watching a
great film. This is how you should
approach every situation in life
to get the full experience.

THE SECRET OF CHANGE
IS TO FOCUS ALL OF
YOUR ENERGY, NOT ON
FIGHTING THE OLD, BUT
ON BUILDING THE NEW.

SOCRATES

◆

If you're interested in finding out more
about our books, find us on Facebook
at SUMMERSDALE PUBLISHERS and follow
us on Twitter at @SUMMERSDALE.

WWW.SUMMERSDALE.COM